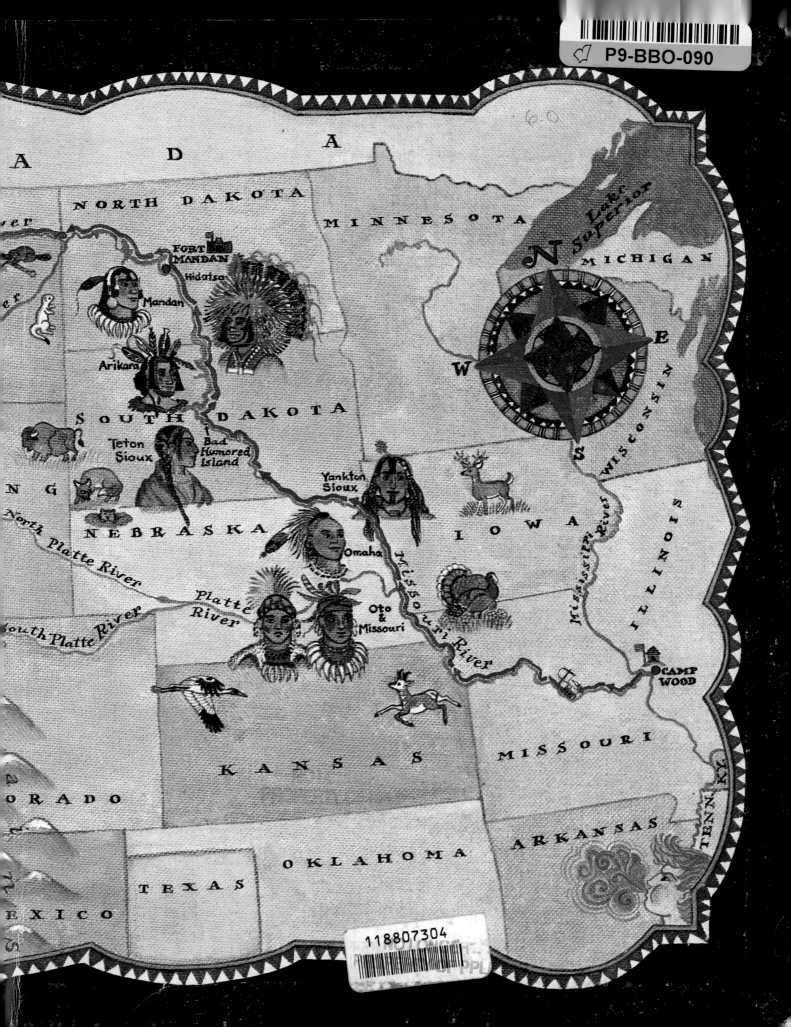

P9-BBO-090

118807304

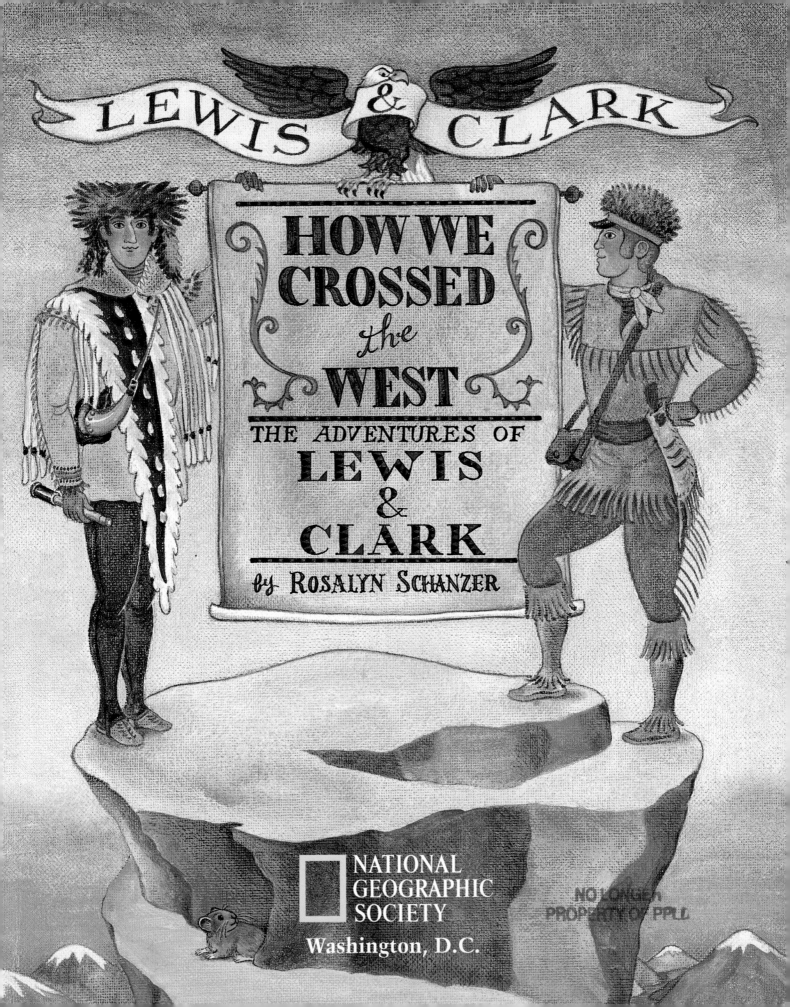

LEWIS & CLARK

HOW WE CROSSED the WEST

THE ADVENTURES OF LEWIS & CLARK

by ROSALYN SCHANZER

NATIONAL GEOGRAPHIC SOCIETY

Washington, D.C.

NO LONGER PROPERTY OF PPLD

J
917.8042
S299h

For Steve

A NOTE FROM THE AUTHOR

I am grateful to the late Arlen Large,
past president of the Lewis and Clark Trail Heritage Foundation,
for reviewing the manuscript and illustrations and providing
helpful comments; Robert Doerk, also a past president of the foundation,
and Curt Johnson at Fort Clatsop National Memorial, for their research
contributions; and Carl Mehler and Joseph Ochlak at the
National Geographic Society for their guidance in making the map.
While I was reading the journals of Meriwether Lewis, William Clark,
and other members of the Corps of Discovery, I was intrigued by
the vivid language they used to describe their remarkable expedition to the
Pacific Coast. I wanted to tell the story in their own words as much as I could,
but sometimes their inventive spelling, 19th-century expressions,
random capitalizations, and long, detailed accounts seemed too difficult for a
young audience to follow. I therefore put together the most exciting passages
from the journals, sometimes shortening sentences or linking the observations
of two or three explorers to clarify the narrative. After much discussion with
expert Arlen Large and my editor Barbara Brownell, spelling was
updated, accuracy confirmed, and when a term was hard to understand
or needed explanation, a word was added in brackets.

The words of Lewis are identified by ℒ

Clark's words by 𝒞

The words of other party members by ☞

I hope that at some time readers will find for themselves the thrill
of reading the original journals mentioned on p. 47, and experience again
the excitement of the Voyage of Discovery.

Copyright © 1997 Rosalyn Schanzer

All rights reserved. Reproduction of the whole or any part
of the contents is prohibited without written permission from the
National Geographic Society, 1145 17th Street, N.W., Washington, D.C. 20036.
   The Society is supported through membership dues and income from the
sale of its educational products. Call 1-800-NGS-LINE for more information.
Visit our website at www.nationalgeographic.com.
Distributed by Publishers Group West. For information call 1-800-788-3123.

Library of Congress Cataloging-in-Publication Data
Schanzer, Rosalyn.
How we crossed the West : the adventures of Lewis & Clark /
Rosalyn Schanzer.
   p.   cm.
ISBN 0-7922-3738-2
1. Lewis and Clark Expedition (1804-1806) 2. Lewis, Meriwether,
   1774-1809. 3. Clark, William, 1770-1838.   I. Title.
   F592.7.S1255 1997
   917.804'2—dc21   96-6585

Printed in the United States of America

Recycled paper ♲

PROPERTY OF
KES PEAK LIBRARY DISTRICT
P.O. BOX 1579
COLORADO SPRINGS, CO 80901

NEARLY 200 YEARS AGO when the United States was a young nation, President Thomas Jefferson sat in the White House thinking. Far beyond the 17 states he led, and farther still beyond the muddy Mississippi River, lay another world, a world of mystery.

Where did its wild and untamed rivers go? What kinds of people and what strange new plants and animals lived along the distant shores? For 20 years, he had dreamed of ways to find a water route leading westward through this unknown land.

One day the President called his private secretary, Captain Meriwether Lewis, into his office and made a most unusual offer. What happened next is told in real words that were written long ago....

MERIWETHER LEWIS to WILLIAM CLARK

Washington, D.C.
June 19, 1803

Dear Clark,

President Thomas Jefferson and the Congress of the United States wish to explore those western rivers which may run all the way across North America to the western ocean, and they have asked me to conduct the passage.

The aims are to meet and begin trading with Indian tribes, to discover new plants and animals, and to make new maps.

My friend, could you join with me to lead this enterprise with all its dangers, its fatigues, and its honors?

Pray let me know what you decide as early as possible.

Your friend & Humble Servant,

Meriwether Lewis.

Louisville, Kentucky
July 18, 1803

Dear Lewis,

I received by yesterday's mail your letter, the contents of which I read with much pleasure. I will cheerfully join you in this rewarding endeavor, and I shall arrange my matters as well as I can to undertake such a trip.

With every sincerity and friendship,

Wm Clark

BUILDING THE KEELBOAT

PITTSBURGH PA.

Design for A sail-bearing Keelboat
55 feet long

by Wm Clark

The person who contracted to build my boat by July 20, 1803, failed. The boat-builders were a set of drunkards; as an instance of their tardiness, they were 12 days in preparing my poles and oars. Not until August 31 was my boat completed. She was instantly loaded. ✒

LOADING THE BOAT

WHITE WAMPUM 5 LBS

EPSOM SALTS

12. oz Opium 10 LBS

Small Cheap Looking Glasses

TENTS

PARCHED CORN

15 Powder Horns & Pouches

BLUE BEADS

30 Calico Shirts

EAR TRINKETS ARM BANDS

15 Rifle Frocks of Waterproof Cloth

200 lbs Best Rifle Powder

150 lbs Portable SOUP

ROCK SALT

15 lbs Scissors

LIST OF REQUIREMENTS
1 Mariner's compass
4 Tin blowing trumpets
24 Iron spoons
1 Cheap portable microscope
1 Instrument for measuring made of tape
6 Papers of ink powder
Mosquito curtains
4 Metal pens
15 Rifles
1 lb. Blistering ointments
2 Crayons
1 Pair pocket pistols, secret triggers
30 Shirts of strong linen
6 Copper kettles
4 Gross fishing hooks assorted
2 Pick axes

FOR THE INDIAN TRADE
Silver peace medals for Indian chiefs
30 Gallons of spirits
50 lbs. Spun tobacco
2 doz. Tinsel tassels
100 Burning glasses
6 Paper small bells
Glass beads, assorted colors
12 Red silk handkerchiefs

A FEW ORIGINAL MEMBERS OF OUR CORPS OF DISCOVERY

JOHN ORDWAY
Top sergeant at Camp Wood, Illinois. Signed on during winter to join permanent party. Ordered to keep a journal in case Lewis and Clark's records get lost.

GEORGE DROUILLARD
Civilian man of much merit. Uncommon skill as a hunter and woodsman, can pursue the faintest tracks. Mother a Shawnee Indian. Interpreter, also knows hand talk.

YORK
Faithful slave of William Clark. Large and powerful, only black member of expedition. Clark's playmate as a child on a Virginia plantation.

PIERRE CRUZATTE
Private. Also a professional riverman. Blind in one eye. Creole, with Omaha Indian mother. Plays the fiddle with great gusto.

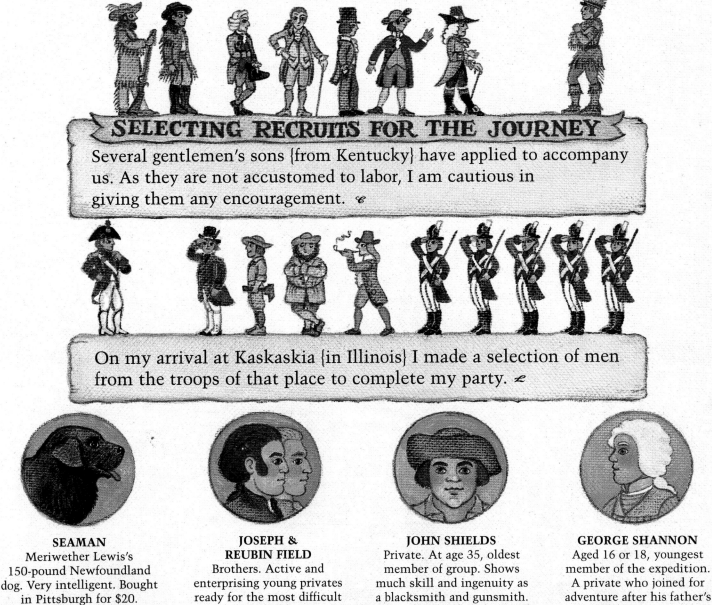

SELECTING RECRUITS FOR THE JOURNEY

Several gentlemen's sons {from Kentucky} have applied to accompany us. As they are not accustomed to labor, I am cautious in giving them any encouragement. *C*

On my arrival at Kaskaskia {in Illinois} I made a selection of men from the troops of that place to complete my party. *C*

SEAMAN
Meriwether Lewis's 150-pound Newfoundland dog. Very intelligent. Bought in Pittsburgh for $20.

JOSEPH & REUBIN FIELD
Brothers. Active and enterprising young privates ready for the most difficult tasks. Selected by Clark in Kentucky.

JOHN SHIELDS
Private. At age 35, oldest member of group. Shows much skill and ingenuity as a blacksmith and gunsmith.

GEORGE SHANNON
Aged 16 or 18, youngest member of the expedition. A private who joined for adventure after his father's death in Ohio.

MAY 14, 1804
CAMP WOOD NEAR ST. LOUIS

Set out at 4 o'clock p.m. in the presence of many of the neighboring inhabitants, and proceeded on under a gentle breeze up the Missouri. ⚬

OUR JOURNEY BEGINS

MAY 15
Saw a number of goslings today on the shore. ⚬

JUNE 4
Our mast got fast on the limb of a sycamore tree and it broke very easy. ⚬

JUNE 5
York swam to the sandbar to gather greens for our dinner. ℰ

JUNE 17
The ticks and mosquitoes are very troublesome. ℰ

We stopped to dine under some trees near the high land. In a few minutes caught three very large catfish, one nearly white. A quart of oil came out of the surplus fat of one fish. Turkeys, geese, and a beaver caught. Great numbers of deer are seen feeding on young willows on the sandbars of the river. Men in high spirits.

Discovered a village of small animals that burrow in the ground. The village covers about four acres and contains great numbers of holes on the top of which those little prairie dogs sit erect. They make a whistling noise when alarmed and step into their holes. ✎

Before sunrise I set out with 6 of my best hunters. I do not exaggerate when I estimate the number of buffalo to amount to 3,000. We found the antelope extremely shy and watchful. Their flight appeared as rapid as the flight of birds! ✎

At sunset a part of the Oto and Missouri nations came to camp. Among those Indians, six were chiefs. We sent them some roasted meat. In return they sent us watermelons. Captain Lewis shooting the air gun a few shots astonished those natives! ℰ

Could not find the Omaha Indians; those people have not returned from their buffalo hunt. The ravages of the smallpox {which swept off 400 men and women and children} has reduced this nation. ℰ

To the Grand Chief of the Yankton Sioux we gave a flag and wampum with a hat and chief coat. After dinner we made a large fire and all the young men prepared themselves for a war dance. The Sioux live by the bow and arrow, some making a vow never to retreat, let the danger be what it may. The warriors are very much decorated with paint, porcupine quills, and feathers. ℰ

TROUBLE

Raised a flagstaff and met in council with about 50 or 60 Teton Sioux. Gave a medal, a laced uniform coat, and a cocked hat with a feather to the chief called Black Buffalo. Second Chief Partizan stated he had not received enough presents, and began insulting us.

His soldiers seized a pirogue {boat} and said we must leave it with them. Our captains told them we must go on and would not be stopped. The warriors said they would follow us and kill us. Then they drew their arrows, but our men instantly pointed the swivel guns in the boats toward them. This impressed them and they withdrew.

We proceeded on and anchored off a willow island I call Bad Humored Island, as we were in a bad humor.

The next morning we went on shore with the chiefs, who appeared to make up and be friendly. The pipe of peace was raised and they put before us the most delicate parts of a dog which they had been cooking. Sioux think dog a great dish, used on all festivals.

Ten men began to beat the tambourine and their women came forward carrying scalps and trophies of war. They proceeded to dance the war dance with great cheerfulness.

OCTOBER 9, 1804

Many {Arikaras} came to view us all day, much astonished at my black servant. This nation never saw a black man before; all flocked around him and examined him from top to toe. By way of amusement he told them that he had once been a wild animal and to convince them he showed them feats of strength. The children would follow him, and when he turned toward them and roared they would run from him and holler and pretend to be terrified and afraid.

The Arikaras are the best-looking, cleanest Indians I have
ever seen on the voyage. Their men are tall and well-
proportioned, their women small and industrious. They
raise great quantities of corn, beans, simmins {squash},
and also tobacco. Those Indians are not fond of spirits or
liquor of any kind. They observed that it would make
them fools, and no man could be their friend who tried to
lead them into such follies. ℰ

BUILDING FORT MANDAN

On October 24, 1804, we saw one of the Grand Chiefs of the Mandans out hunting. With great cordiality we smoked the pipe. Every day curious men, women, and children flocked down to see us. These are the most friendly Indians inhabiting the Missouri. ℭ

On November 2, we went down the river to look for a proper place to winter and found a place well supplied with wood. The next morning we commenced the building of Fort Mandan, named in honor of our neighbors, on the east bank of the Missouri. ☞

A Mr. Toussaint Charbonneau came down to see us, and wished to be hired as an interpreter. This man has a wife called Sacagawea, who is about 14 or 15 years of age. She is from the Shoshoni {Snake} nation and was captured by Hidatsa Indians when she was about 10. The Shoshonis live by the Rocky Mountains and own many horses. Charbonneau informs us that his squaw will tell these Indians of our need for horses to carry baggage over the mountains. She is with child. ✍

A WINTER OF EXCESSIVE COLD

DECEMBER 7, 1804
Captain Lewis took 15 men and joined the Indians, who were killing buffalo on horseback. Three men frostbit badly today.

DECEMBER 17, 1804
Very cold. The thermometer at sunrise stood at 45° below 0.

JANUARY 10, 1805
The mercury this morning stood at 40° below 0. An Indian man came in who had stayed out all night without fire, and very thinly clothed. This man was not the least injured. Those people bear more cold than I thought it possible.

MARCH 29, 1805
Observed extraordinary dexterity {skill} of the Indians in jumping from one cake of ice to another for the purpose of catching buffalo. Many cakes of ice are not two feet square. ᴇ

JANUARY 1, 1805

We suffered 16 men with their music to visit the village for the purpose of dancing by the request of the chiefs. I found them very pleased, particularly with one of the Frenchmen who danced on his hands with his head downward. ᴄ

FEBRUARY 11, 1805

This evening Sacagawea was delivered of a fine boy. This was her first child and Mr. Jessaume informed me that a small portion of the rattle of a rattlesnake had never failed to hasten a birth. Having such a rattle, I gave it to him. He administered two rings of it broken in small pieces and added to water. Whether this medicine was the cause or not, she had not taken it ten minutes before the baby was born. ᴌ

APRIL 7, 1805
WE CONTINUE ON

At 4 p.m. we dismissed the barge and crew with orders to return to St. Louis with our dispatches to the government, letters to our friends, and several articles to the President of the United States.

Our party to continue the Voyage of Discovery now consists of 33 individuals including the wife of Charbonneau and her infant son, Jean Baptiste {called Pomp}. Our vessels are 6 small canoes and 2 large pirogues. We are now about to penetrate a country on which the foot of civilized man has never trodden. ✍

TWO NARROW ESCAPES

MAY 14, 1805

A sudden squall hit the white pirogue and Charbonneau—who is perhaps the most timid waterman in the world—dropped the rudder, crying to his god for mercy and almost turning the boat topsy-turvy. In this pirogue was every article necessary to insure the success of our journey. Repeated orders could not bring him to do his duty until the bowsman, Cruzatte, threatened to shoot him instantly. The boat righted but was filled with water. The waves were running high. Cruzatte ordered two of the men to throw out water with some kettles while he and two other men rowed her ashore. Sacagawea, whose fortitude was equal to any person on board, caught and saved most of the light articles which were washed overboard.

In the evening, the men discovered a large brown {grizzly} bear, and six hunters went out to attack him. Each put a bullet through him, two through both lungs. In an instant this monster ran at them with open mouth. Two more men shot him, but this stopped his motion for a moment only. The men ran for the river and the bear pursued.

The bear was so close that the men threw aside their guns and threw themselves into the river, though the bank was 20 feet high. The animal plunged into the water a few feet behind the second man. One of those still on shore shot the bear through the head and finally killed him. ✎

THE GREAT FALLS OF THE MISSOURI

JUNE 13 AND 14, 1805

My ears were saluted with the sound of a tremendous roaring and I saw spray rise above the plain like a column of smoke. I hurried to gaze on the grandest sight I ever beheld, an enormous cascading fall of water, beating with great fury. ✐

JUNE 27, 1805

Hail about the size of pigeons' eggs covered the ground to one inch and a half. As the balls struck the ground they would rebound to the height of 20 or 30 feet before they touched again. If one had struck a man on the naked head, it would have killed him. The men saved themselves by getting under a canoe. ✐

WE MEET THE SHOSHONIS

AUGUST 17, 1805

A fair cold morning. I saw Indians on horseback coming toward me. Sacagawea danced for the joyful sight and made signs to me that they were her nation.

The Great Chief Cameahwait of this nation proved to be the brother of Sacagawea! He is a man of influence, good sense, and easy manners.

We spoke to the Indians about our want of horses to cross the mountains. They said the route was unfavorable, with immense waterfalls and steep cliffs, and that there were no deer, elk, or game to eat. ℰ

LATE SUMMER, 1805
CROSSING THE BITTERROOT MOUNTAINS

On August 30, we set out on our route. Traversed some of the worst roads that a horse ever passed on the sides of steep and stony mountains, some covered with snow. ✃

Several horses fell, some crippled. Frazer's horse fell near a hundred yards into the creek, but to our astonishment, he arose to his feet but little injured. ✍

Found water nearly boiling hot in places where it spouted from the rocks. One of the Indians made a hole to bathe. ✃

Several times compelled to kill a colt for our men and selves to eat for want of meat. Encamped one night at a bold running creek I called Hungry Creek as we had nothing to eat. ✍

Woke this morning and to our great surprise we were covered with snow. Our moccasins froze; the ink freezes in my pen. ✍

To our inexpressible joy, saw a prairie 60 miles distant. We should reach its borders tomorrow. Spirits of the party much revived, as they are weak for want of food. ✍

RUNNING THE RAPIDS

Having triumphed over the mountains at last, a man of the Nez Percé {Pierced Noses} escorted us to the Grand Chief's lodge. With great cheerfulness, their Chief Twisted Hair drew a map on white elkskin to show the rivers beyond his camp.

We determined to go where the best timber was and commenced building five canoes. We have adopted the Indian method of burning out the canoes.

OCTOBER 1805

Built dugout canoes and set out past many bad rapids between rugged rocks and cliffs 200 feet high. One canoe split open and sank; another turned over. A great many articles lost. All our powder, some bedding, and half our food prepared in the Indian way wet. Nothing to eat but roots.

After 17 days, this great roaring river compressed between 2 rocks not 45 yards wide. Determined to pass this horrid swelling, boiling, and whorling in every direction, we rode with great velocity and passed safe, to the astonishment of all the Indians who viewed us from atop the rocks. ☞

ONWARD TO OREGON

OCTOBER 1805

I went on shore and found the Indians much frightened in their lodges. They thought we were not men but birds that fell from the clouds. As soon as they saw Sacagawea, they understood our friendly intentions, as no woman ever accompanies a war party. ✐

The river widens and becomes a beautiful gentle stream of about half a mile wide. Great numbers of harbor seals about. ✐

The fleas are very troublesome and our men can't get rid of them. They strip off their clothes and kill the fleas during which time they remain naked. ✐

Salmon trout, which we had fried in a little bear's oil, I thought one of the most delicious fish I have ever tasted. ✐

The Chinook Indians flatten the heads of the female children and of many male children also. Heads of many infants are two inches thick on the forehead and thinner still higher. ✐

Chiluckitequaw canoes ride the highest waves. They are very light and heads of animals are carved on the raised bow. ✐

High cliff of rocks. I saw one of the mountain goats. It had thick wool and long, coarse hair on the back resembling bristles. ✐

A chief opened his medicine bag and showed me 14 fingers, which he said were the fingers of different enemies taken in war. ✐

Slept very little last night. The swans, geese, brants {kind of goose}, and etc. were immensely numerous and their noise horrid. ✐

CLOSER & CLOSER TO

NOVEMBER 7, 1805

We were encamped under a high hill when the morning fog cleared off. Ocean in view! Oh! The joy. This great Pacific Ocean which we have been so long anxious to see, and the roaring noise made by waves breaking on rocky shores may be heard distinctly. ℰ

The seas rolled and tossed the canoes in such a manner that several of our party were seasick. ℰ

Five Indians came down in a canoe with fish to sell. One had on a sailor's jacket and pantaloons he got from white people. ℰ

THE GREAT PACIFIC!

Eleven days of rain, and most disagreeable. Cannot get out to hunt, return to a better position, or proceed on. ✺

Immense swells from the main ocean immediately in front of us. All the men who wish to see the main ocean prepare themselves to set out early tomorrow morning. ✺

Labels around the border:

North American Badger

Snow Goose

Wild Licorice

Cranberry

Bighorn Sheep

Prickly Pear

Porcupine

Wapato

Bullsnake

Sagebrush

Passenger Pigeon

Sitka Spruce

RETURN JOURNEY

Lewis and Clark wintered near the Pacific Ocean and left for home on March 23, 1806. Indian friends pointed out a fast route through the mountains, and then the party split into two groups for a while to explore the Marias and Yellowstone Rivers.

Many adventures followed. Lewis and three of his party battled eight Blackfeet Indians who were trying to steal their guns and horses. One-eyed Cruzatte mistook Lewis for an elk and shot him in the britches. The Mandan chief Big White joined the explorers to visit President Jefferson. And finally, nearing home, the men discovered that they had been given up for dead long ago.

On Sunday, September 21, 1806, in the village of St. Charles near St. Louis, the jubilant explorers were greeted by cheering crowds. They had been gone for more than two years and four months.

ACCOMPLISHMENTS

* Traveled through 7,689 miles of wilderness to the Pacific Ocean and back, and made detailed maps of fertile prairies, towering mountains, raging rivers, and primeval forests.

* Discovered scores of plants and animals formerly unknown to science.

* Chronicled the customs, languages, and artifacts of more than 50 proud eastern and western Indian nations and established peaceful relations with almost all of them.

* Explored the newly acquired Louisiana Purchase and enabled a young United States to claim the Oregon region of North America.

* Changed the destiny of North America by opening the West to fur traders, mountain men, and others from east of the Mississippi.

* Overcame enormous hardship with imagination and good humor, and carried out every one of President Jefferson's goals to run the most well-managed expedition of exploration in written history.

HOW THIS BOOK WAS MADE

When Lewis and Clark and their Corps of Discovery crossed the continent, they wrote a remarkable series of letters, notebooks, and journals describing in detail every day of their journey and all of the events leading up to it.

Each account was so intriguing that before I knew it, I had read about 40 books, including the letters and journals, as well as other sources recommended by Lewis and Clark experts. Most of the quotes come from Reuben Gold Thwaites's *Original Journals of the Lewis and Clark Expedition* (6 Vols.), 1969. Some other sources are Nicholas Biddle's *The Expedition of Lewis and Clark* (2 Vols.), 1966; Milo Quaife's *The Journals of Captain Meriwether Lewis and Sergeant John Ordway*, 1916; and Donald Jackson's *Letters of the Lewis and Clark Expedition With Related Documents* (1 Vol.), 1978.

To make the pictures, I used descriptions from the journals, and looked at drawings and paintings of Indians and landscapes by artist/adventurers Karl Bodmer and George Catlin. Models of the various boats made by R.C. Boss and on display in Fort Clatsop National Memorial in Astoria, Oregon, were helpful source material as were photographs of Indian artifacts, geographical features, and animals.

Finally, I chose the quaint painting style of American folk artists of the period as a fitting accompaniment to the explorers' picturesque writing style. To further enhance the antique look of the art, I painted on rough canvas with watered-down acrylics and then added colored pencil to bring out the texture.

Missouri Beaver

Osage Orange

Candlefish

Bitterroot

Sage Grouse

Prairie Apple

Elk

California Condor

Salmonberry

118807304

PROPERTY OF
PIKES PEAK LIBRARY DISTRICT
P.O. BOX 1579
COLORADO SPRINGS, CO 80901

THE *Route* OF
LEWIS & CLARK
WESTWARD FROM THE
MISSISSIPPI TO THE PACIFIC OCEAN
MAY 1804 ~ NOVEMBER 1805

miles
0   50   100   150   200

0 50 100 150 200 250 300
kilometers

MAP SHOWS PRESENT DAY
STATE BORDERS